BLAZERS

WEAPONS OF WAR

WEAPONS OF THE

Modern Day

by Matt Doeden

Content Consultant:
Raymond L. Puffer, PhD
Retired Historian
United States Air Force

WITHDRAWN

Reading Consultant:
Barbara J. Fox
Reading Specialist
North Carolina State University

Capstone
press

Mankato, Minnesota

Blazers is published by Capstone Press,
151 Good Counsel Drive, P.O. Box 669, Mankato, Minnesota 56002.
www.capstonepress.com

Library of Congress Cataloging-in-Publication Data
Doeden, Matt.
    Weapons of the modern day / by Matt Doeden.
    p. cm. — (Blazers. Weapons of war)
    Includes bibliographical references and index.
    Summary: "Describes modern-day military weapons, including guns, explosives, and
vehicles" — Provided by publisher.
    ISBN-13: 978-1-4296-2333-9 (hardcover)
    ISBN-10: 1-4296-2333-0 (hardcover)
    1. Military weapons — Juvenile literature. I. Title.
UF500.D684 2009
623.4 — dc22   2008030852

Editorial Credits
Mandy Robbins, editor; Alison Thiele, set designer; Kyle Grenz, book designer;
    Jo Miller, photo researcher

Photo Credits
AP Images/Abdelhak Senna, 8–9 (soldier); Adam Butler, 12–13; Esteban Felix, 18–19
Corbis/Bettmann, 6
DEFENSEIMAGERY.MIL/TSGT Andy Dunaway, USAF, 29 (Apache)
Getty Images Inc./AFP/Jack Pritchard, 22; AFP/Michael Kappeler, 14–15; Business Wire, 27
iStockphoto/Carl Anderson, cover (M16), 17 (M16); Ramon Purcell, 10, 16 (AK47)
Newscom, 9 (M16), 16 (XM-15); AFP/Earnie Grafton, 11; Getty Images/AFP/HO, 4–5
Photo by Ted Carlson/Fotodynamics, 23 (AIM), 23 (GP bombs), 23 (mines), 24–25
Shutterstock/Brent Wong, 17 (M2); Vartanov Anatoly, 16 (sniper rifle); Vladimir Melnik, 17
    (AK47 on tripod)
U.S. Air Force photo, cover (F-22), 26, 29 (Predator); Master Sgt Andy Dunaway, 29 (F16)
U.S. Navy Photo, 23 (RPGs); by MC2 James R. Evans, 28; by Missile Defense Agency, 21;
    by PH1 Ted Banks, 29 (M1A1)
Wikimedia/United States Army, 16 (M9); United States Federal Government, 17 (M4)

1 2 3 4 5 6 14 13 12 11 10 09

Table of Contents

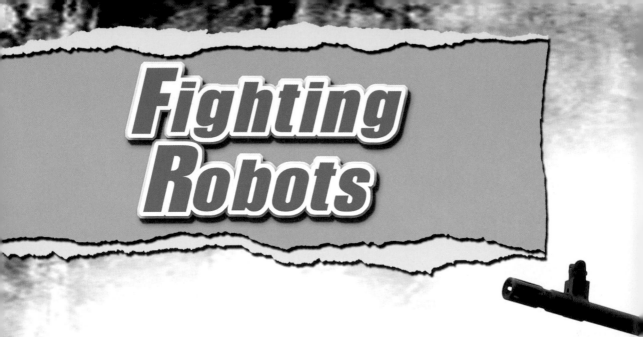

Fighting Robots

A U.S. *SWORDS* machine rolls across the battlefield. It turns and fires. These machines keep U.S. soldiers out of harm's way.

SWORDS – a remote-controlled robotic combat soldier, formally called the Special Weapons Observation Remote Direct-Action System

Talon
S.W.O.R.D.S.

nuclear bomb explosion

Every military wants the most accurate weapons. From robots to *nuclear bombs*, weapons are becoming better than ever.

nuclear bomb — a powerful bomb that destroys large areas and leaves behind dangerous particles called radiation

Serious Firepower

The M16 is a popular *automatic* rifle for many militaries. Some models shoot more than 800 bullets per minute.

automatic — having the ability to shoot more than one bullet with a single squeeze of the trigger

non-military M16

Israeli military M16

WEAPON FACT

The Russian military uses the AK47.
It is similar to an M16.

AK47

SAW

The Squad Automatic Weapon (SAW)
is a lightweight machine gun. It can shoot
1,000 bullets per minute.

M2 heavy machine gun

WEAPON FACT

U.S. soldiers call the M2 "Ma Deuce."

The U.S. Army uses the M2 heavy machine gun against aircraft and small vehicles. The M2 shoots bullets that punch through tough metal *armor*.

armor — a protective metal covering on military vehicles

Sniper rifles pick off targets from a distance. Long barrels and *scopes* make them very accurate. The M110 SASS hits targets more than .5 mile (.8 kilometer) away.

barrel

scope — a device mounted to a gun that makes distant objects appear larger

scope

German sniper rifle

Firepower

sniper rifle

M9 pistol

AK47

XM15 Bushmaster

M2 vehicle machine gun

AK47 on tripod

M4 rifle

M16 rifle

Extreme Explosives

RPG-7

Powerful explosives destroy helicopters, tanks, and other large targets. Rocket-propelled grenades (RPGs) streak across the sky. They explode on contact.

WEAPON FACT

The GBU-28 "Bunker Buster" is a 5,000-pound (2,268-kilogram) bomb. It blasts into underground shelters.

Ballistic *missiles* are rockets that carry *warheads*. Cruise missiles have wings and an engine. They can change direction in flight.

missile — a weapon that can travel long distances

warhead — the explosive part of a missile

Standard Missile 2

Bombs cause major damage too.
Laser-guided bombs (LGBs) use laser
beams to locate targets. Nuclear bombs
can destroy entire cities.

Paveway II
laser-guided bomb

Missiles, Mines, and Grenades

AIM sidewinder missile

rocket-propelled grenades

GP bombs in bomb bay

MK 62 Quickstrike mines

Vicious Vehicles

Military vehicles are powerful forces. Tanks rumble over almost any surface. The M1 Abrams tank has heavy armor and a huge gun.

M1A2 Abrams tank

F-22 Raptor
fighter plane

Military planes streak across the
sky. Fighters fire missiles at air and land
targets. Bombers drop powerful explosives.

WEAPON FACT

The Predator is a remote-controlled plane. It can spy on an enemy or fire a missile at a target.

Predator

Navies fight with fleets of ships.
Aircraft carriers are huge floating airports.
Cruisers are small and fast. Submarines
lurk below the ocean surface. All ships
carry guns, missiles, and *torpedoes*.

torpedo — an explosive missile that
travels underwater

USS *Abraham Lincoln*
aircraft carrier

Fighting Vehicles

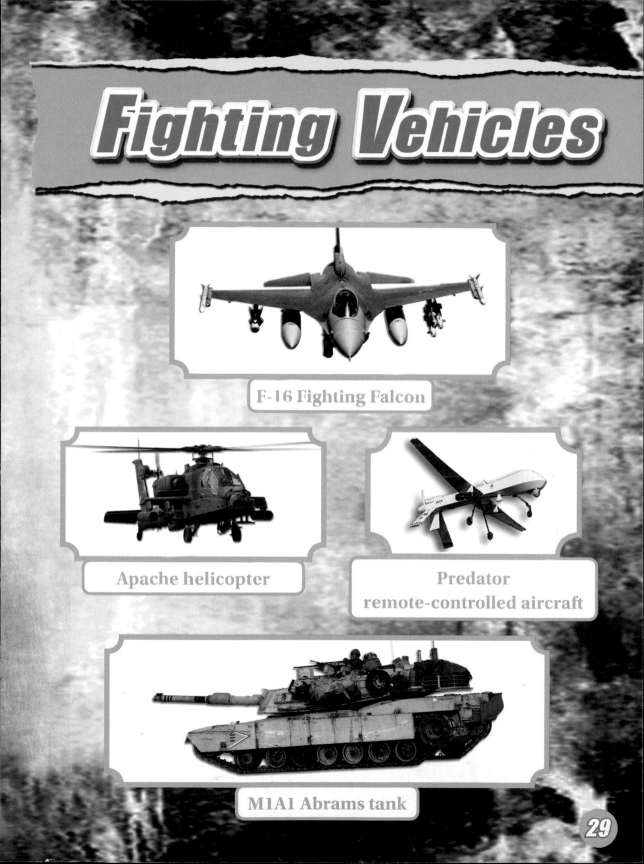

F-16 Fighting Falcon

Apache helicopter

Predator
remote-controlled aircraft

M1A1 Abrams tank

Glossary

armor (AR-muhr) — a protective metal covering

automatic (aw-tuh-MAT-ik) — able to shoot more than one bullet with a single squeeze of the trigger

fleet (FLEET) — a group of ships that sail together

missile (MISS-uhl) — an explosive weapon that can fly or travel long distances

nuclear bomb (NOO-klee-ur BOM) — a powerful explosive that destroys large areas; nuclear bombs leave behind harmful elements called radiation.

scope (SKOHP) — a device mounted to a gun that makes distant objects appear larger and easier to see

SWORDS (SORDS) — a remote-controlled robotic combat soldier, formally known as the Special Weapons Observation Remote Direct-Action System

torpedo (tor-PEE-doh) — an explosive missile that travels underwater

warhead (WOR-hed) — the explosive part of a missile or rocket

Read More

Braulick, Carrie A. *U.S. Air Force Fighters.* Military Vehicles. Mankato, Minn.: Capstone Press, 2006.

Graham, Ian. *Military Technology.* New Technology. Mankato, Minn.: Black Rabbit Books, 2008.

Hamilton, John. *Weapons of the 21st Century.* War in Iraq. Edina, Minn.: Abdo, 2004.

Internet Sites

FactHound offers a safe, fun way to find educator-approved Internet sites related to this book.

Here's what you do:

1. Visit *www.facthound.com*

2. Choose your grade level.

3. Begin your search.

This book's ID number is 9781429623339.

FactHound will fetch the best sites for you!

Index